Praise the King of Heaven

*Songs of Worship, Hymns, and Gospel Classics
Arranged for Festival Choir*

BY TOM FETTKE

SINGER'S EDITION

> PLEASE NOTE: Copying of this product is not covered by CCLI licenses.
> For CCLI information call 1-800-234-2446.

Lillenas PUBLISHING COMPANY
KANSAS CITY, MO 64141

COPYRIGHT © 1993 BY PILOT POINT MUSIC.
ALL RIGHTS RESERVED.   LITHO IN U.S.A.

CONTENTS

BE THOU MY VISION	23
BRIGHT AND MORNING STAR	79
The Lily of the Valley	
It's Just Like His Great Love	
COME, EVERY ONE WHO IS THIRSTY	75
GLORIOUS IS THY NAME	38
Glorious Is Thy Name *(Mozart)*	
Glorious Is Thy Name *(McKinney)*	
GOD LEADS US ALONG	19
HIS EYE IS ON THE SPARROW	68
HIS NAME IS WONDERFUL, with	32
My Wonderful Lord	
JESUS IS LORD OF ALL	10
I WANT TO BE LIKE JESUS, with	53
Lord, Be Glorified	
O TO BE LIKE THEE, with	36
Lord, Lay Some Soul upon My Heart	
PRAISE, MY SOUL, THE KING OF HEAVEN	5
PRAISE TO THE LORD, THE ALMIGHTY, with	89
Praise God, from Whom All Blessings Flow	
SHINING LIGHT	64
Find Us Faithful	
Song for the Nations	
SING HALLELUJAH	49
SPIRIT OF GOD, DESCEND UPON MY HEART	56
THE BOND OF LOVE	84
THE FOUNDATION	59
The Solid Rock	
The Church's One Foundation	
THE HONORS OF THY NAME	26
O for a Thousand Tongues to Sing	
Blessed Be the Name	
TRAVELING ON	15
I Feel Like Traveling On	
We'll Work till Jesus Comes	
WHAT A DAY THAT WILL BE	43
YOUR LOVE COMPELS ME, with	86
And Can It Be?	

Praise, My Soul, the King of Heaven

HENRY F. LYTE

MARK ANDREWS
Arr. by Tom Fettke

With great strength ♩ = ca. 112

Cued notes optional (if tessitura is too high for alto and/or bass)

Praise, my soul, the King of heav-en;
To His feet your trib-ute bring.
Ran-somed, healed, re-stored, for-giv-en, Ev-er-more His prais-es sing. Al-le-

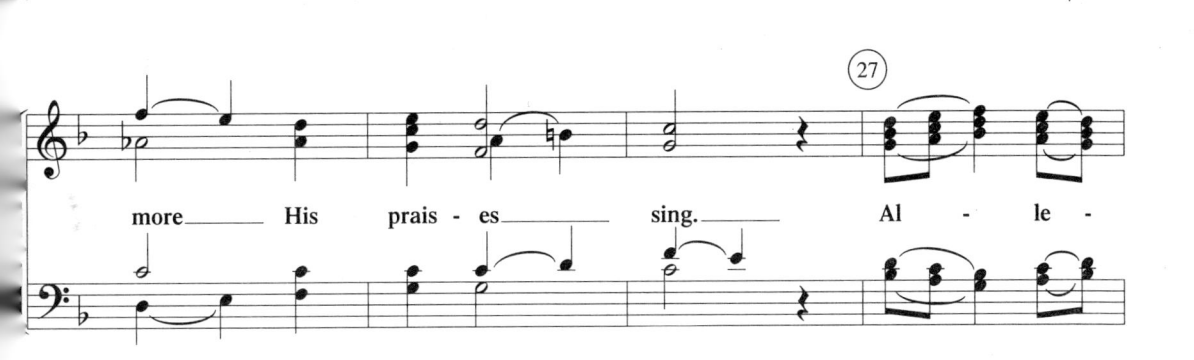

Copyright © 1958 (Renewed) G. Schirmer, Inc. (ASCAP). International copyright secured.
All rights reserved. Used by permission of G. Schirmer, Inc.

Jesus Is Lord of All

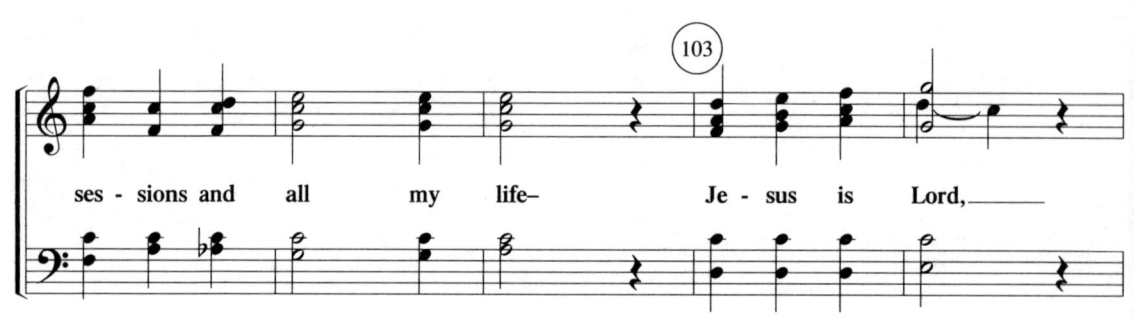
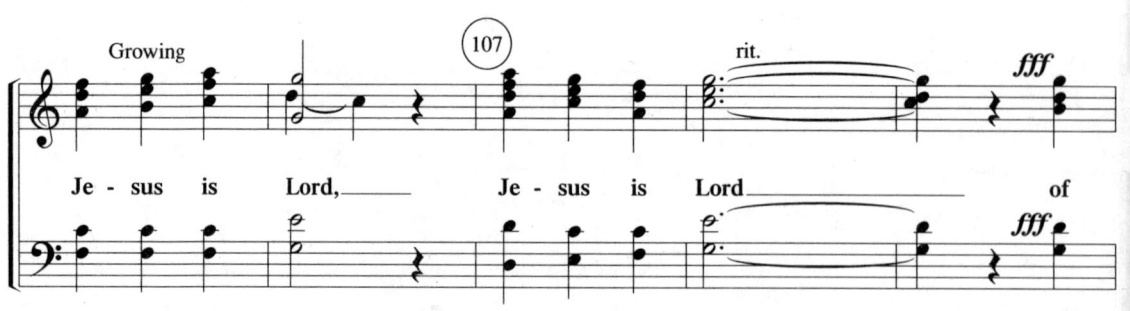
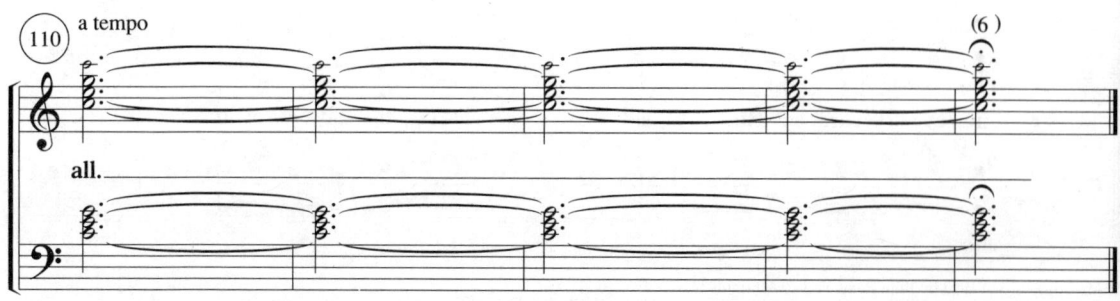

15

Traveling On

Arr. by Tom Fettke

God Leads Us Along
A Cappella

Be Thou My Vision

TRADITIONAL IRISH HYMN
Translated by Mary E. Byrne
Versified by Eleanor H. Hull

TRADITIONAL IRISH MELODY
Arr. by Tom Fettke

Earnestly ♩ = ca. 84

Ladies unison
Be Thou my Vi - sion, O Lord of my heart;

Men unison
Naught be all else to me, save that Thou art—

Ladies div. ... *Unison*
Thou my best thought, by day or by night,

Men unison ... rit. ... a tempo
Wak - ing or sleep - ing, Thy pres - ence my light.

Be Thou my Wis - dom, and Thou my true Word;

I ev - er with Thee and Thou with me, Lord;

Arr. copyright © 1993 by Pilot Point Music. All rights reserved.
Administered by Integrated Copyright Group, Inc., P.O. Box 24149, Nashville, TN 37202.

26

The Honors of Thy Name

Arr. by Tom Fettke

*Arr. copyright © 1993 by Pilot Point Music. All rights reserved.
 Administered by Integrated Copyright Group, Inc., P.O. Box 24149, Nashville, TN 37202.

**Arr. copyright © 1993 by Pilot Point Music. All rights reserved.
 Administered by Integrated Copyright Group, Inc., P.O. Box 24149, Nashville, TN 37202.

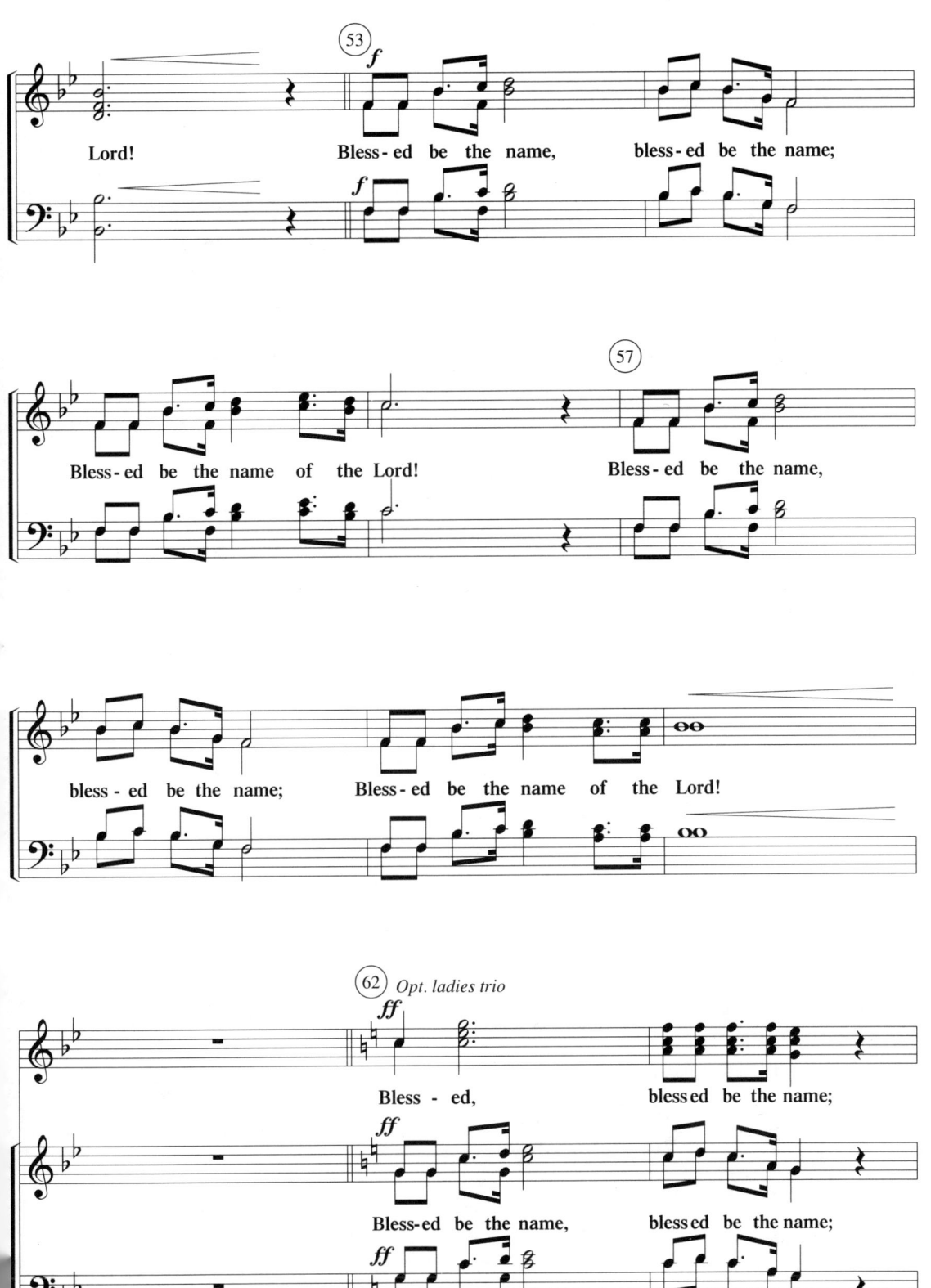

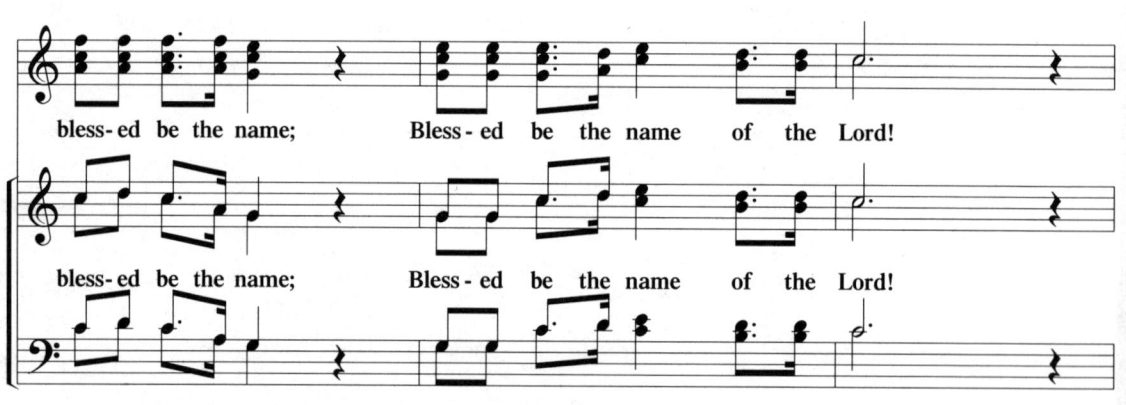

His Name Is Wonderful
with
My Wonderful Lord

Arr. by Tom Fettke

*Copyright © 1938, renewed 1966, arr. © 1993 by Lillenas Publishing Co. All rights reserved.
Administered by Integrated Copyright Group, Inc., P.O. Box 24149, Nashville, TN 37202.

36

O to Be Like Thee
with
Lord, Lay Some Soul upon My Heart
A Cappella

Arr. by Tom Fettke

*"O to Be Like Thee" (Thomas Chisholm - William J. Kirkpatrick)

*Arr. copyright © 1993 by Pilot Point Music. All rights reserved.
Administered by Integrated Copyright Group, Inc., P.O. Box 24149, Nashville, TN 37202.

rit.   *mp*

wan - d'ring sin - ner to find. Lord,

11. *"Lord, Lay Some Soul upon My Heart" (Leon Tucker - Ira D. Sankey)

a tempo

lay some soul up - on my heart, And

love that soul through me; And

15. rit.

may I al - ways do my part To

Slower   *pp*

win that soul for Thee, for Thee.

*Arr. copyright © 1993 by Pilot Point Music. All rights reserved.
Administered by Integrated Copyright Group, Inc., P.O. Box 24149, Nashville, TN 37202.

Glorious Is Thy Name

Arr. by Tom Fettke

With majesty ♩ = ca. 122

*"Glorious Is Thy Name" (W. A. Mozart)

Glo - rious is Thy name, Al - might - y Lord;

Glo - rious is Thy name, is Thy name, O Lord;

Glo - rious is Thy name, Glo - ri - ous is Thy name, Al - Al -

---

*Arr. copyright © 1993 by Pilot Point Music. All rights reserved.
Administered by Integrated Copyright Group, Inc., P.O. Box 24149, Nashville, TN 37202.

17
might - - - -
might - y, glo - rious is Thy name, O Lord; Glo - rious
might - y, glo - rious
20
- - - y,
is Thy name, O Lord, glo - rious is Thy name, O Lord.
is Thy name, is Thy name,
24
ff
Glo - rious is Thy name, Al - might - y Lord.
ff
28
*"Glorious Is Thy Name" (B. B. McKinnney)
mf Unison
Bless - ed Sav - ior, we a - dore Thee; We Thy love and grace pro - claim.
mf Unison
32
Thou art might - y; Thou art ho - ly. Glo - rious is Thy match - less name!

36
Stronger
Div.
Glo - ri - ous, Glo - ri - ous,
Div.
40
1
2
Glo - rious is Thy name, O Lord! name, O Lord!
46
f
Great Re - deem - er, Lord and Mas - ter,
f
50
Light of all e - ter - nal days, Let the saints of
ev - 'ry na - tion Sing Thy just and end - less praise!

54
ff Optional descant
Glo - ri - ous, Glo - ri - ous,
ff
Glo - ri- ous, Glo - ri- ous,
ff
58
1
2
Glo- rious is Thy name, O Lord! name,
1
2
Glo- rious is Thy name, O Lord! name,
62
O Lord!
O Lord!

66 Remain *ff*

Glo - rious is Thy name, is Thy name, O Lord;

Glo - rious is Thy name. Bless - ing and hon - or

be to God, for - ev - er and ev - er - more;

76 Bless - ing and hon - or be to God, for - ev - er and ev - er -

80 more; Bless - ing and hon - or for - ev - er - more.

What a Day That Will Be

J. H.

JIM HILL
Arr. by Tom Fettke and Randy Smith

With anticipation ♩. = ca. 67

There is com - ing a day when no heart - aches shall come— No more clouds in the sky, no more tears to dim the eye. All is peace for - ev - er more on that hap - py gold - en shore. What a

Copyright © 1955. Renewed 1983, Ben Speer Music/SESAC. All rights reserved.
Used by permission of Integrated Copyright Group, Inc.

day, glo-ri-ous day that will be! What a
be, will be!

day that will be when my Je-sus I shall

see, And I look up-on His face— the One who

saved me by His grace. When He takes me by the

hand and leads me through the Prom-ised Land, What a

day, glo-ri-ous day that will be!

Solo (freely)
There'll be no sor-row there, no more bur-dens to bear, No more sick-ness, no pain, no more part-ing o-ver there. And for-ev-er I will be with the One who died for me.

Oo

What a day, glo-ri-ous

day that will be!

What a day that will be when my Je-sus I shall see, And I look up-on His face— the One who saved me by His

grace. When He takes me by the hand and leads me through the Prom-ised Land, What a day, glo-ri-ous day that will be! What a day that will be when my Je-sus I shall see, And I look up-on His face— the One who

Stronger
saved me by His grace, by His grace. When He
85
takes me by the hand and leads me through the Prom - ised
Mel.
Land, What a day, glo - ri - ous
90
Mel.
day that will be! What a day, glo - ri - ous
94
rit.
(6)
day that will be!

Sing Hallelujah

J. H.

JACK HAYFORD
Arr. by Tom Fettke

With great energy ♩ = ca. 120

1st verse: Choir unison melody (soprano part)
2nd verse: Parts as written

1. There has not failed one word of all His prom- ise; All He has spo- ken He has done, just as He said. Stand on His Word, se- cure, un- changed for- ev- er; And sing hal- le- lu- jah! Faith-ful
2. Whirl- winds of change are blow- ing 'cross the na- tions; Storms of con- fu- sion blast and buf- fet all man- kind. Stands Christ, our King, His "peace be still" com- mand- ing; And now, hal- le- lu- jah! I have

Copyright © 1980, 1993 by Pilot Point Music. All rights reserved.
Administered by Integrated Copyright Group, Inc., P.O. Box 24149, Nashville, TN 37202.

God, our Fa - ther!
peace un - end - ing!

3. With haunt-ing doubt or pas-sion of temp-ta - tion,
Sa - tan would sift you and would seek to steal your joy.
Hear Je - sus speak, "I've prayed for you; you'll fail not." And
sing hal - le - lu - jah! I am o - ver-com - ing!

4. When in the fi - 'ry furnace of af - flic - tion
Hell's pow'r would cast you, or some weak-ness lay you low,
Stand on His Word: "I am the Lord, your Heal - er." And
sing hal - le - lu - jah! By His stripes He heals us!

5. Chil - dren of light, the dark-ness fast is gath - 'ring.

Earth's black-est mid-night comes; its last tra-vail be-gins.

Stand in the light— God's Word out-shines the shadows;

Sing hal-le-lu-jah! We've a bright to-mor-row! Sing hal-le-lu-jah! Sing hal-le-lu-jah! Sing hal-le-lu-jah!

Chil-dren of light!
(Hal-le-lu-jah!)

I Want to Be Like Jesus
with
Lord, Be Glorified

Arr. by Tom Fettke

Smoothly ♩ = ca. 80

⑦ *"Lord, Be Glorified" (Bob Kilpatrick)

In my life, Lord, be glo-ri-fied, be glo-ri-fied.

⑪ rit.   A little faster ♩ = ca. 86

In my life, Lord, be glo-ri-fied to-day.

⑯ **"I Want to Be Like Jesus" (Thomas Chisholm - David Ives)

mp Solo or unison choir

I have one deep, su-preme de-sire, That I may be like

⑳

Je-sus. To this I fer-vent-ly as-pire, That I may be like

㉔ A little faster ♩ = ca. 90

accel. *mf*

Je-sus. I want my heart His throne to be,

㉘ A little slower ♩ = ca. 86

rit.

So that a watch-ing world may see His like-ness shin-ing

*Copyright © 1978 by Bob Kilpatrick Music, P.O. Box 2383, Fair Oaks, CA 95628.
All rights reserved. Used by permission.

**Copyright © 1945, renewed 1973, arr. © 1993 by Lillenas Publishing Co. All rights reserved.
Administered by Integrated Copyright Group, Inc., P.O. Box 24149, Nashville, TN 37202.

forth in me. I want to be like Je-sus.

Faster ♩ = ca. 90

O per-fect life of Christ, my Lord! I want to be like Je-sus. My rec-om-pense and my re-ward, That I may be like Je-sus. His Spir-it fill my hun-g'ring soul, His pow-er all my life con-trol;

47
mf
My deep - est prayer, my high - est goal, That I may be like
51
Je - sus. In my heart, Lord,
mf
I want to be like Je - sus. In my heart, Lord,
55
mp
59 Slower ♩ = ca. 72
mp
great rit.
I want to be like Je - sus. I want to be like
rit.
a tempo
decresc. and rit.
(6)
Je - sus.

Spirit of God, Descend Upon My Heart
A Cappella

GEORGE CROLY

FREDERICK C. ATKINSON
Arr. by Tom Fettke

Prayerfully

Spir - it of God, de - scend up - on my heart.
Wean it from earth; through all its puls - es move.
Stoop to my weak - ness, might - y as Thou art.
And make me love Thee as I ought to love.

Arr. copyright © 1993 by Pilot Point Music. All rights reserved.
Administered by Integrated Copyright Group, Inc., P.O. Box 24149, Nashville, TN 37202.

57

17 *Soprano and Alto* *mf*
Hast Thou not bid us love Thee, God and King?

Tenor and Bass *mf*

21
All, all Thine own— soul, heart and strength and mind!

25 *cresc.*
I see Thy cross— there teach my heart to cling.

cresc.

29 *f* *decresc.*
O— let me seek Thee, and O let me find.

f *decresc.*

33 *mp*
Teach me to love Thee as Thine an-gels love,

One ho-ly pas-sion fill-ing all my frame;

Ten. only

(41) *mf cresc.*
The bap-tism of the heav'n-de-scend-ed Dove—

(45) *f* — *decresc.*
My heart an al-tar, and Thy love the flame.

(49) *rit. pp*
Thy love the flame.

My heart an al-tar, and Thy love the flame.

The Foundation

Arr. by Tom Fettke

a - tion By water and the Word. From heav'n He came and sought her To be His ho-ly bride; With His own blood He bought her, And for her life He died.

rit. and decresc. *more rit.*

A little slower ♩ = ca. 92
Unison **mp**

E - lect from ev - 'ry na - tion, Yet one o'er all the earth; Her char-ter of sal - va - tion: One Lord, one faith, one birth; One

Unison **mp**

44 *cresc. poco a poco*

ho - ly name she bless - es, Par - takes one ho - ly food, And

48 continue to cresc. *Div.* slight rit. Faster ♩ = ca. 100 *f*

to one hope she press - es, With ev - 'ry grace en - dued.

continue to cresc. *Div.* *f*

2 *f* 55

'Mid toil and trib - u - la - tion And

2 *f*

59

tu - mult of her war, She waits the con - sum - ma - tion Of

63

peace for - ev - er - more; Till with the vi - sion glo - rious Her long-ing eyes are blest, And the great Church vic-to-rious Shall be the Church at rest. Yet she on earth hath un-ion With God, the Three in One, And mys-tic sweet com-mun-ion With those whose rest is won. O hap-py ones and ho-ly! Lord, give us grace that

63

Shining Light

Arr. by Tom Fettke

With great sincerity ♩ = ca. 69

*"Find Us Faithful" (Jon Mohr)

O may all who come be-hind us find us faith-ful; May the fire of our de-vo-tion light their way. May the foot-prints that we leave Lead them to be-lieve, And the lives we live in-spire them to o-bey. O may all who come be-hind us find us

A little slower

*Copyright © 1987 by Jonathan Mark Music (c/o Gaither Copyright Management) and Birdwing Music/BMG Songs, Inc. All rights reserved. Used by permission.

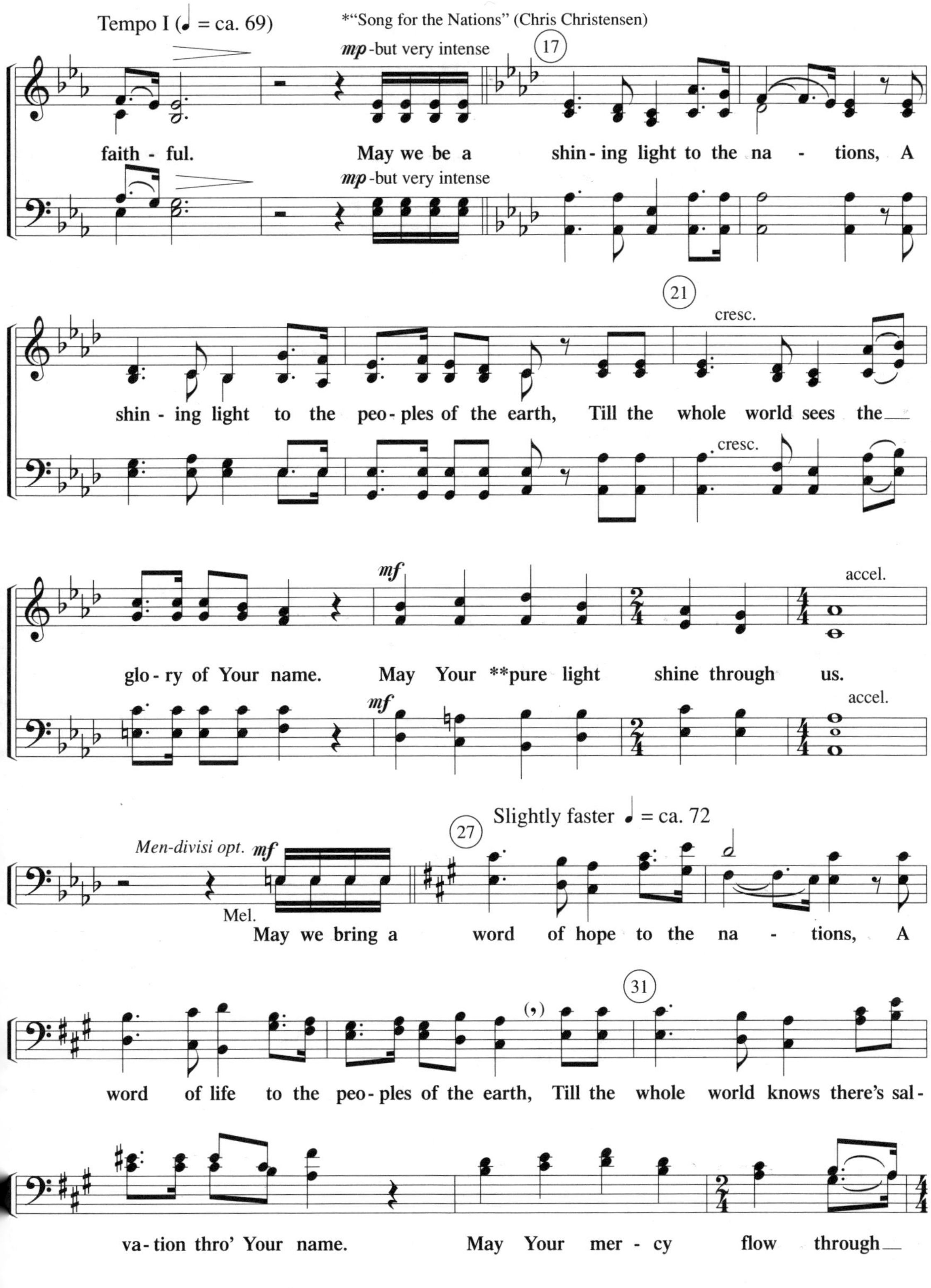

us. May we sing a song of joy to the nations, A song of praise to the peoples of the earth, Till the whole world rings with the prais-es of Your name. May Your song be sung through us. May your king - dom come to the na - tions, Your

67

will be done in the peo-ples of the earth,____ Till the whole world knows that____ Je-sus Christ is Lord. May Your king-dom come, May Your king-dom come, Stronger May Your king-dom come in____ us. A - men.____

His Eye Is on the Sparrow

MRS. C. D. MARTIN

CHARLES H. GABRIEL
Arr. by Tom Fettke

Brightly ♪ = ca. 144

I sing be-cause I'm hap-py, I sing be-cause I am free; For His eye is on the spar-row, And I know He watch-es me.

Slower ♪ = ca. 130

Unison

Why should I feel dis-cour-aged? Why should the shad-ows

Arr. copyright © 1993 by Pilot Point Music. All rights reserved.
Administered by Integrated Copyright Group, Inc., P.O. Box 24149, Nashville, TN 37202.

19
come?___ Why should my heart___ be lone-ly___
23
Div.
And long for heav'n and home___ When Je - sus is___ my
Div.
por - tion?___ My con - stant Friend___ is He.___ His
27
eye is on___ the spar - row,___ And I know He watch - es
31
rit.
(,)
me.___ His eye is on the spar - row,___ And I
(,)

Faster ♪ = ca. 144
35
know He watch - es me. I sing be - cause I'm
hap - py, I sing be - cause I am free; For His
39
rit.
eye is on the spar - row, And I know He watch - es
decresc.
Slower ♪ = ca. 130
44
3
rit.
me.
47
Slower ♪ = ca. 120
Solo
mp
"Let not your heart be trou - bled," His ten - der words I

hear;_____ And rest-ing on His good-ness,_____ I lose my doubt and fear._____ Tho' by the path_____ He lead-eth_____ But one step I_____ may see,_____ His eye is on_____ the spar-row,_____ And I know He watch-es

Oo_____

Ah_____

63
rit.
decresc.
me. His eye is on the spar - row, And I
rit.
decresc.
Ah
decresc.
Slower ♪ = ca. 112
mp
accel. and cresc.
know He watch-es me.
68
Faster ♪ = ca. 136
mf
When-ev - er I am tempt - ed, when-ev - er clouds a -
mf
72
rise, When songs give place to sigh - ing,

When hope with-in me dies, I draw the clos-er to Him; From care He sets me free. His eye is on the spar-row, And I know He watch-es me. His eye is on the spar-row, And I know He watch-es me. I sing be-cause I'm

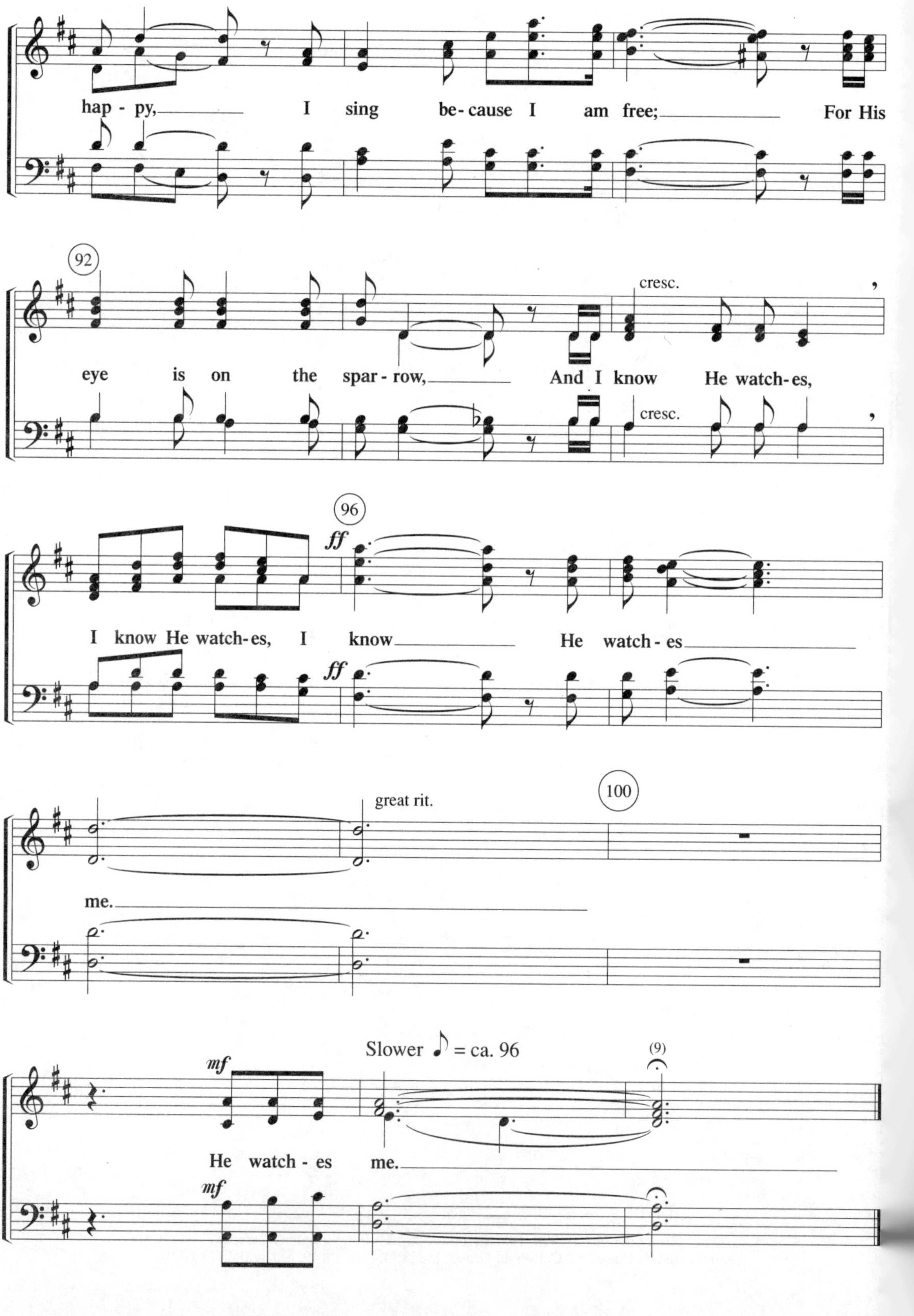
hap - py, I sing be- cause I am free; For His
92
eye is on the spar - row, And I know He watch- es,
cresc.
cresc.
96
ff
ff
I know He watch- es, I know He watch - es
great rit.
100
me.
Slower ♪ = ca. 96
mf
mf
(9)
He watch - es me.

Come, Every One Who Is Thirsty

L. J. R.

LUCY J. RIDER
Arr. by Tom Fettke

Flowing ♩ = ca. 84

mp Choir unison or solo

Come, ev-'ry one who is thirst-y in spir-it.

Come, ev-'ry one who is wea-ry and sad.

Come to the foun-tain; there's full-ness in Je-sus—

All that you're long-ing for. Come and be glad.

Choir
mp

"I will pour wa-ter on him who is thirst-y; I will pour

Arr. copyright © 1976, 1993 by Pilot Point Music. All rights reserved.
Administered by Integrated Copyright Group, Inc., P.O. Box 24149, Nashville, TN 37202.

floods up-on the dry ground. O-pen your heart for the gift I am bring-ing. While you are seek-ing Me, I will be found." Child of the king-dom, be filled with the Spir-it! Noth-ing but full-ness thy long-ing can meet. 'Tis the en-due-ment for

77

life and for ser-vice. Thine is the prom-ise, so cer-tain, so sweet!

(29) Tempo I (♩ = ca. 84)

"I will pour wa-ter on him who is thirst-y; I will pour floods up-on the dry ground.

(33) O-pen your heart for the gift I am bring-ing. While you are seek-ing Me, I will be found."

(38) a tempo
mf Unison
"I will pour wa-ter on

him who is thirst - y; I will pour floods up -
on the dry ground.
42
cresc.
Div.
O - pen your heart for the
Slower ♩ = ca. 78
rit.
decresc.
gift I am bring - ing.
While you are seek - ing Me,
46 Slower ♩ = ca. 70
rit.
mp
(4)
I will be found.
While you are seek - ing Me,
rit.
a tempo
(6)
I will be found."
Come, come.

Bright and Morning Star

Arr. by Tom Fettke

Majestic ♩ = ca. 82   Brightly ♩ = ca. 112   *"The Lily of the Valley" (Charles Fry - William Hayes)

I've found a friend in Je-sus; He's ev-'ry-thing to me. He's the fair-est of ten thou-sand to my soul. The Lil-y of the Val-ley, in Him a-lone I see All I need to cleanse and make me ful-ly whole. In sor-row He's my com-fort; in trou-ble He's my stay. He tells me ev-'ry care on Him to roll. He's the Lil-y of the Val-ley, the

*Arr. copyright © 1993 by Pilot Point Music. All rights reserved.
Administered by Integrated Copyright Group, Inc., P.O. Box 24149, Nashville, TN 37202.

Bright and Morn-ing Star. He's the fair-est of ten thou-sand to my soul. He's the

23 *rit. poco a poco* *Div.*

Lil-y of the Val-ley, the Bright and Morn-ing Star. He's the

decresc. New tempo, slower ♩ = ca. 96 *mp* **28** *"It's Just like His Great Love"* (Edna Worrell - Clarence Strouse)

fair-est of ten thou-sand to my soul. A friend I have, called

32

Je-sus, Whose love is strong and true And nev-er fails, how-

cresc. *slight rit.* *mf*

e'er 'tis tried— No mat-ter what I do. I've

*Arr. copyright © 1993 by Pilot Point Music. All rights reserved.
Administered by Integrated Copyright Group, Inc., P.O. Box 24149, Nashville, TN 37202.

sinned a-gainst this love of_ His; But when I knelt to pray, Con-fess-ing all my guilt to Him, The sin-clouds rolled a-way._ It's just like Je-sus to roll the clouds a-way. It's just like Je-sus to keep me day by day. It's just like Je-sus all a-long the way. It's just like His great love._ O

82

54 I could sing for-ev-er Of Jesus' love di-vine— Of

58 all His care and ten-der-ness For this poor life of mine. His
cresc. *mf*

62 *Duet*
Alto love His love is in and o-ver all, And wind and waves o-
Tenor mf His love is in and

66 bey When Jesus whis-pers, "Peace, be still!" And
rit. *sub. mf*
sub. mf

A little faster ♩ = ca. 116 *Choir* *71*
f
rolls the clouds a-way. It's just like Jesus to roll the clouds a-way. It's
Div.
Div. f

75
just like Jesus to keep me day by day. It's just like Jesus

all a-long the way. It's just like His great love.

It's just like Jesus to roll the clouds a-way. It's just like Jesus to keep me day by day. It's just like Jesus

all a-long the way. It's just like His great

love, re-deem-ing love.

The Bond of Love
A Cappella

O. S.

OTIS SKILLINGS
Arr. by Tom Fettke

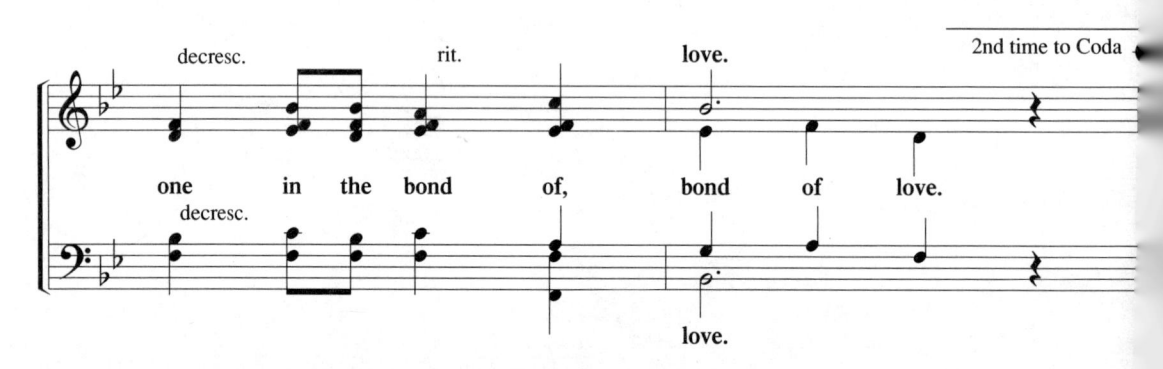

We are one in the bond of love. We are one in the bond of love. We have joined our spirits with the Spirit of God; We are one in the bond of, bond of love.

love.

love.

Copyright © 1971 by Lillenas Publishing Co. All rights reserved.
Administered by Integrated Copyright Group, Inc., P.O. Box 24149, Nashville, TN 37202.

(9) *Solo (or section)* *mp* *a tempo* *cresc.*
Love through Christ has brought us to-geth-er, Melt-ing our hearts as one.

mp a tempo *cresc.*
Loo, loo, loo, loo, loo, loo, loo, loo, loo, loo, loo, loo.

(13) *mf*
By God's Spir-it we are u-nit-ed,

No breath *mf*
Loo, loo, loo, loo, loo, loo,

rit. and decresc.
One through His bless-ed Son.

D.S. al Coda

loo, loo, loo, loo, loo. We are

mp

CODA
pp Slowly   *rit.*
One in the bond of love.

Your Love Compels Me
with
And Can It Be?

Arr. by Tom Fettke

With great warmth ♩ = ca. 72

*"And Can It Be?" (Charles Wesley - Thomas Campbell)

A - maz - ing love! How can it be That Thou, my God, shouldst die for me?

**"Your Love Compels Me" (Doug Holck)

Unison

Your love com - pels me, Lord, to give as You would give, To speak as You would speak, to live as You would live. Your love com - pels me, Lord,

---

*Copyright © 1982, 1993 by Pilot Point Music. All rights reserved.
Administered by Integrated Copyright Group, Inc., P.O. Box 24149, Nashville, TN 37202.

**Arr. copyright © 1993 by Pilot Point Music. All rights reserved.
Administered by Integrated Copyright Group, Inc., P.O. Box 24149, Nashville, TN 37202.

87

to see as You would see, To serve as You would serve,

cresc. and slight accel. A little faster ♩ = ca. 79 *mf*

to be what You would be. Your love com - pels me, Lord,

to give as You would give, To speak as You would speak,

Div.

to live as You would live. Your love com - pels me, Lord,

Unison

to see as You would see, To serve as You would serve,

cresc. and slight accel. A little faster ♩ = ca. 82 *f*

to be what You would be. Your love com - pels me, Lord,

51
to give as You would give, To speak as You would speak,
55
cresc.
Div.
to live as You would live. Your love com - pels me, Lord,
decresc. and rit. poco a poco
59
Unison
to see as You would see, To serve as You would serve,
64
Slowly, freely ♩ = ca. 68
Div.
mp
to be what You would be. Your love com - pels me, Lord,
rit.
a tempo
pp
to be what You would be.

Praise to the Lord, the Almighty
with
Praise God, from Whom All Blessings Flow

Arr. by Tom Fettke

Intense worship ♩ = ca. 76

Unison **mp** -but intense

⑦ *"Praise God, from Whom All Blessings Flow"
(Thomas Ken - Louis Bourgeois)

Praise God, from whom all bless-ings flow. Praise Him, all crea-tures here be-low. Praise Him a-bove, ye heav'n-ly host. Praise Fa-ther, Son, and Ho-ly Ghost.

⑮ Faster ♩ = ca. 128

㉑ **"Praise to the Lord, the Almighty" (Joachim Neander - W. Sterndale)

Men unison

mf Praise to the Lord, the Al-might-y, the King of cre-

---

*Arr. copyright © 1993 by Pilot Point Music. All rights reserved.
Administered by Integrated Copyright Group, Inc., P.O. Box 24149, Nashville, TN 37202.

**Arr. copyright © 1993 by Pilot Point Music. All rights reserved.
Administered by Integrated Copyright Group, Inc., P.O. Box 24149, Nashville, TN 37202.

a - tion! O my soul, praise Him, for He is thy health and sal - va - tion.

Div. **mf** All ye who hear, Now to His tem - ple draw near;

Join me in glad ad - o - ra - tion.

rit. poco a poco

Slower ♩ = ca. 96 **mp** Praise to the Lord, who o'er all things so won - drous - ly

Div. **mp**

rit. reign - eth, *a tempo* Shel - ters thee un - der His

wings, yea, so gent-ly sus-tain - eth!

57 *a tempo*
Hast thou not seen How thy de-
Hast thou not, hast thou not seen
Hast thou not seen

slight rit. **63** *a tempo* *decresc.*
sires all have been Grant-ed in what He or-

rit. **68** Faster ♩ = ca. 116
dain - eth?

72 Unison *f* — Sing cued notes only if tessitura is too high
Praise to the Lord! O let all that is in me a-dore

Him! All that hath life and breath, come now with prais-es be-fore Him! Let the "a-men" Sound from His peo-ple a-gain; Glad-ly for-ev-er, for ev-er and ev-er a-dore the Lord!